"FEAR NOT, F

AM WITH YOU; BE

NOT DISMAYED,

FOR I AM YOUR

GOD. I WILL

STRENGTHEN YOU,

YES, I WILL HELP

YOU, I WILL

UPHOLD YOU

WITH MY

RIGHTEOUS RIGHT

HAND."

— ISAIAH 41:10

"LORD MY GOD, I CALLED TO YOU FOR HELP, AND YOU HEALED ME." — PSALM 30:2

"Come to me, all you who are weary and burdened, and I will give you rest." — Matthew 11:28

"IS ANYONE AMONG YOU SICK? LET THEM CALL THE ELDERS OF THE CHURCH TO PRAY OVER THEM AND ANOINT THEM WITH OIL IN THE NAME OF THE LORD. AND THE PRAYER OFFERED IN FAITH WILL MAKE THE SICK PERSON WELL; THE LORD WILL RAISE THEM UP. IF THEY HAVE SINNED, THEY WILL BE FORGIVEN."

— JAMES 5:14-15

"'But I will restore you to health and heal your wounds,' declares the Lord..." — Jeremiah 30:17

"MY SON, GIVE ATTENTION TO MY WORDS; INCLINE YOUR EAR TO MY SAYINGS. DO NOT LET THEM DEPART FROM YOUR EYES; KEEP THEM IN THE MIDST OF YOUR HEART; FOR THEY ARE LIFE TO THOSE WHO FIND THEM, AND HEALTH TO ALL THEIR FLESH." — PROVERBS 4:20-22

"A CHEERFUL HEART IS GOOD MEDICINE, BUT A CRUSHED SPIRIT DRIES UP THE BONES." — PROVERBS 17:22

"And my God will meet all your needs according to the riches of his glory in Christ Jesus." — Philippians 4:19

"...You restored me to health and let me live. Surely it was for my benefit that I suffered such anguish. In your love you kept me from the pit of destruction; you have put all my sins behind your back." — Isaiah 38:16-17

"HE GIVES POWER TO THE WEAK, AND TO THOSE WHO HAVE NO MIGHT HE INCREASES STRENGTH...THOSE WHO WAIT ON THE LORD SHALL RENEW THEIR STRENGTH; THEY SHALL MOUNT UP WITH WINGS LIKE EAGLES, THEY SHALL RUN AND NOT BE WEARY, THEY SHALL WALK AND NOT FAINT." —

ISAIAH 40:29,31

"HE HIMSELF BORE OUR SINS IN HIS BODY ON THE TREE, THAT WE MIGHT DIE TO SIN AND LIVE TO RIGHTEOUSNESS. BY HIS WOUNDS YOU HAVE BEEN HEALED." — 1 PETER 2:24

"THIS IS MY COMFORT IN MY AFFLICTION, THAT YOUR PROMISE GIVES ME LIFE." — PSALM 119:50

"HE HEALS THE BROKENHEARTED AND BINDS UP THEIR WOUNDS." — PSALM 147:3

"BELOVED, I PRAY THAT ALL MAY GO WELL WITH YOU AND THAT YOU MAY BE IN GOOD HEALTH, AS IT GOES WELL WITH YOUR SOUL." — 3 JOHN 1:2

"And God will wipe away every tear from their eyes; there shall be no more death, nor sorrow, nor crying. There shall be no more pain, for the former things have passed away."
— Revelation 21:4

"LORD, BE GRACIOUS TO US; WE LONG FOR YOU. BE OUR STRENGTH EVERY MORNING, OUR SALVATION IN TIME OF DISTRESS." — ISAIAH 33:2

"THEREFORE CONFESS YOUR SINS TO EACH OTHER AND PRAY FOR EACH OTHER SO THAT YOU MAY BE HEALED. THE PRAYER OF A RIGHTEOUS PERSON IS POWERFUL AND EFFECTIVE." — JAMES 5:16

"PEACE I LEAVE WITH YOU; MY PEACE I GIVE YOU. I DO NOT GIVE TO YOU AS THE WORLD GIVES. DO NOT LET YOUR HEARTS BE TROUBLED AND DO NOT BE AFRAID." — JOHN 14:27

"MY FLESH AND MY HEART MAY FAIL, BUT GOD IS THE STRENGTH OF MY HEART AND MY PORTION FOREVER." —

PSALM 73:26

"BUT FOR YOU WHO FEAR MY NAME, THE SUN OF RIGHTEOUSNESS SHALL RISE WITH HEALING IN ITS WINGS. YOU SHALL GO OUT LEAPING LIKE CALVES FROM THE STALL." — MALACHI 4:2

"JESUS WENT THROUGH ALL THE TOWNS AND VILLAGES, TEACHING IN THEIR SYNAGOGUES, PROCLAIMING THE GOOD NEWS OF THE KINGDOM AND HEALING EVERY DISEASE AND SICKNESS." — MATTHEW 9:35

"AND THE PEOPLE ALL TRIED TO TOUCH HIM, BECAUSE POWER WAS COMING FROM HIM AND HEALING THEM ALL." — LUKE 6:19

"The LORD is my shepherd, I lack nothing. He makes me lie down in green pastures, he leads me beside quiet waters, he refreshes my soul. He guides me along the right paths for his name's sake. Even though I walk through the darkest valley, I will fear no evil, for you are with me; your rod and your staff, they comfort me."

— Psalm 23:1-4

"Trust in the LORD with all your heart, and lean not on your own understanding. In all your ways submit to him, and he will make your paths straight. Do not be wise in your own eyes; fear the LORD and shun evil. This will bring health to your body and nourishment to your bones." —

Proverbs 3:5-8

"Do not be anxious about anything, but in everything by prayer and supplication with thanksgiving let your requests be made known to God. And the peace of God, which surpasses all understanding, will guard your hearts and your minds in Christ Jesus."
— Philippians 4:6-7

"NOT ONLY THAT,
BUT WE REJOICE IN
OUR SUFFERINGS,
KNOWING THAT
SUFFERING
PRODUCES
ENDURANCE, AND
ENDURANCE
PRODUCES
CHARACTER, AND
CHARACTER
PRODUCES HOPE..."
— ROMANS 5:3-4

"HEAL ME, O LORD, AND I SHALL BE HEALED; SAVE ME, AND I SHALL BE SAVED, FOR YOU ARE MY PRAISE." — JEREMIAH 17:14

"Have mercy on me, Lord, for I am faint; heal me, Lord, for my bones are in agony." — Psalm 6:2

"Worship the LORD your God, and his blessing will be on your food and water. I will take away sickness from among you..." — Exodus 23:25

"THE RIGHTEOUS CRY OUT, AND THE LORD HEARS THEM; HE DELIVERS THEM FROM ALL THEIR TROUBLES. THE LORD IS CLOSE TO THE BROKENHEARTED AND SAVES THOSE WHO ARE CRUSHED IN SPIRIT." — PSALM 34:17-18

"But he said to me, 'My grace is sufficient for you, for my power is made perfect in weakness.' Therefore I will boast all the more gladly of my weaknesses, so that Christ's power may rest on me." — 2 Corinthians 12:9

"When Jesus came down from the mountainside, large crowds followed him. A man with leprosy came and knelt before him and said, 'Lord, if you are willing, you can make me clean.' Jesus reached out his hand and touched the man. 'I am willing,' he said. 'Be clean!' Immediately he was cleansed of his leprosy."

— Matthew 8:1-3

"Gracious words are a honeycomb, sweet to the soul and healing to the bones." — Proverbs 16:24

"PRAISE THE LORD, MY SOUL, AND FORGET NOT ALL HIS BENEFITS —WHO FORGIVES ALL YOUR SINS AND HEALS ALL YOUR DISEASES, WHO REDEEMS YOUR LIFE FROM THE PIT AND CROWNS YOU WITH LOVE AND COMPASSION." — PSALM 103:2-4

Printed in Great Britain
by Amazon